COOL CAREERS
WITHOUT COLLEGE
FOR PEOPLE WHO LOVE
MUSIC

COOL CAREERS WITHOUT COLLEGE FOR PEOPLE WHO LOVE MUSIC

CARLA MOONEY

ROSEN PUBLISHING®

New York

Published in 2014 by The Rosen Publishing Group, Inc.
29 East 21st Street, New York, NY 10010

Library of Congress Cataloging-in-Publication Data

Mooney, Carla, 1970–
Cool careers without college for people who love music/Carla Mooney.—First edition.
        pages; cm—(New cool careers without college)
Includes bibliographical references and index.
ISBN 978-1-4777-1819-3 (library binding)
1. Music—Vocational guidance—Juvenile literature. I. Title.
ML3928.M65 2013
780.23—dc23

2013012398

Manufactured in the United States of America

CPSIA Compliance Information: Batch #W14YA: For further information, contact Rosen Publishing, New York, New York, at 1-800-237-9932.
A portion of the material in this book has been derived from *Cool Careers Without College for Music Lovers* by Kerry Hinton.

CONTENTS

INTRODUCTION

Have you ever thought about music as a career? If your answer is yes, then this is for you. This book is all about careers in music. It takes all types of people to make music and get it played live and on the radio. Take a look at some of these career options —you might just discover that you want to take the leap into the music industry.

None of the jobs that you will find listed here require a college degree, but they all demand what most jobs do: dedication and patience to see results. You do not even need to know how to play a musical instrument for the majority of these jobs!

You will read about twelve different professions that are associated with music in various ways. Each entry describes a job, the training you may need, and lots of resources for more information. Many of the jobs we discuss can be merged with another job or worked as a second job while you gain experience. You may have never even heard of some of these jobs. Go ahead, read, and find out. You might just discover several exciting career options that you hadn't even thought of before now.

A student learns the functions of sound recording equipment from his instructor. A career in sound engineering can lead to work in the music or movie industry.

CHAPTER 1

PRIVATE MUSIC TEACHER

A good music teacher can inspire a child to a life-long love of music and music-making. Music teachers teach students how to play an instrument. You'll give lessons to kids and adults alike, from brand-new beginners to more experienced musicians. While you'll have to deal with some students who come to lessons because their parents force them, most private music students are eager to learn.

A DAY IN THE LIFE

Private music teachers can work in a variety of places. They may teach in their own home or travel to students' homes. They may also give lessons at a music store, private studio, or similar location. Lessons can last anywhere from thirty minutes to about an hour and often take place once per week. A lesson may be one-on-one, with just the teacher and one student. Other times, lessons are taught in groups, where the teacher has a small group of students at the same time. Music teachers also work with a variety of students, with different ages, backgrounds, and experiences. Some students may be as young as four or five years old and are just beginning to learn how to

At a weekly lesson, a student plays a song he has practiced at home for his teacher. The teacher discusses the music with the student and offers his suggestions for performing the piece.

hold an instrument and read music. Other students may have played an instrument for several years and are working on more challenging pieces of music. Older students may know how to play one instrument but want to learn how to play a second instrument. Because every student is different, music teachers should be flexible and patient. Making the lesson enjoyable is an important part of every music teacher's job. To be successful, they should be able to relate well to students and have an encouraging manner.

INTERVIEW: EIGHT QUESTIONS WITH A MUSIC TEACHER

Fugi Sisca, Batavia Studios, Seven Fields, Pennsylvania

1. HOW LONG HAVE YOU WORKED AS A MUSIC TEACHER? I have worked as a music teacher for over ten years.

2. HOW DID YOU GET THIS JOB? My best friend saw an ad on Craig's List and called me immediately. I had been teaching independently out of my home.

3. DID YOU GO TO COLLEGE FOR THIS JOB? IF SO, WHAT DID YOU MAJOR IN? IF NOT, WHY WAS IT NOT NEEDED? I majored in communications and minored in music and psychology. I use all three in this job extensively. Technically, you do not need to have a degree to teach music.

4. WHAT IS THE BEST PART/UPSIDE OF YOUR JOB? The very best part is watching children learn and enjoy music. My favorite part is when a song that was difficult becomes easy with practice. I like to think that later on in life my students will have the ability to relax, de-stress, and enjoy playing their instrument.

5. WHAT IS THE WORST PART/DOWNSIDE OF YOUR JOB? By far the worst thing is when a student doesn't practice. You want them to have fun with it, but if they don't practice it becomes a drag for everyone involved.

6. WHAT IS A TYPICAL DAY LIKE? A typical day for me is a four- or five-hour shift in the evenings. I work part-time, and the hours are great. Typically, I teach back to back without a break. The main focus is reviewing the students' assigned pieces that they practiced the previous week. I am always looking to see how I can help them improve their skills from where they are. Progress not perfection is my motto.

I teach piano, voice, flute, and beginner guitar. The bulk of my students are piano or voice students. The ages of the students vary from three years old to mature adults. I also have a few students who come to my home and we basically follow the same format.

7. WHAT WORK IS INVOLVED IN GETTING STUDENTS READY FOR RECITALS/COMPETITIONS? For recitals and competition, I like my students to be over prepared. I really put a lot of effort into making sure it is a positive experience for them. We go over the piece many times to make sure the student could practically play it in their sleep. That way if nerves kick in they will still be fluent in the piece. Oftentimes I also have them play their pieces on different pianos to experience the feel or sound of other instruments. We also play the piece in front of other teachers or students to have the experience of playing in front of others. If there is anything I can think of to help the student improve their performance or make the experience easier and more fun I definitely do it. It is very rewarding to see a student work that hard on a piece and then watch them perform it. It is definitely my favorite part of teaching.

8. ANYTHING ELSE WE SHOULD KNOW? I'd also like to add that there are many careers in music, and if you have a passion for music you should definitely pursue it as a career. It is creative, fun, and not the least bit stressful. I personally know many people who have made a career in music. It may take some work to figure out what your niche is but that is true in any field. Please do not listen to people who tell you otherwise. It is a complete fallacy that you will never make a living at it.

Most private music teachers work for themselves and make their own hours. If they work for a music store or studio, they may follow the store's hours and schedule for lessons. No matter what hours you set as a music teacher, you should be reliable and dependable. Students depend on you to be at lessons where and when you schedule them, so try to avoid cancelling lessons or showing up late.

WHAT EDUCATION AND TRAINING DO MUSIC TEACHERS NEED?

No particular education is required to be a music teacher. If you want to work as a music teacher, it is essential that you can play the instrument or instruments that you want to teach. You should be able to teach students different techniques of playing and

A music teacher adjusts how a student holds the bow of her violin. Music teachers often demonstrate the proper way to hold instruments and fingers for beginning students.

how to read music. Therefore, you will need to have extensive training on specific instruments, either through a music school or private lessons. You'll also need to be patient and enthusiastic even if your students don't practice or don't want to be there.

SALARY EXPECTATIONS

Most private music teachers work on their own and set their own rates. Others work for a music store or studio whose policies set pay rates. Most teachers are paid by the hour or per lesson. Rates depend on the instrument being taught and the teacher's experience. Teachers who are more experienced and teach experienced musicians earn more. In a music store or studio, the teacher is either paid per student, in a weekly salary, or a combination of the two methods.

CAREER OUTLOOK

There are always students looking for music teachers. Once a teacher gathers a few students who are happy with his or her instruction, word of mouth can quickly spread to potential new students. Because music teachers decide their own hours, many teachers can work another job or career and give lessons part-time to interested students. As teachers take on more students and establish a good reputation in the community, they can charge higher rates. Eventually, a private music teacher may decide to open a private music studio, where he or she can hire other private music teachers.

EXTRA INFO

No two students are alike, and even the same student will have different lessons from week to week. To be successful, a private music teacher needs to be flexible and able to work with all types of people and personalities. If a teacher is able to create a warm, nurturing, and interesting environment for learning about music, he or she will be successful in developing a new generation of music lovers.

FOR MORE INFORMATION

ORGANIZATIONS

American Federation of Musicians
New York Headquarters
1501 Broadway, Suite 600
New York, NY 10036
(212) 869-1330
Web site: http://www.afm.org/about

Music and Entertainment Industry Student Association
   (MEISA)
1900 Belmont Boulevard
Nashville, TN 37212
(615) 460-6946
Web site: http://www.meisa.org

Music Teachers National Association (MTNA)
441 Vine Street, Suite 3100
Cincinnati, OH 45202-3004
(513) 421-1420 or (888) 512-5278
Web site: http://www.mtna.org

National Association for Music Education (NAfME)
1806 Robert Fulton Drive
Reston, VA 20191

(703) 860-4000 or (800) 336-3768
Web site: http://www.nafme.org

BOOKS

Blanchard, Bonnie, and Cynthia Blanchard Acree. *Making Music and Enriching Lives: A Guide for All Music Teachers*. Bloomington, IN: Indiana University Press, 2007.
In this book, you will find specifics not only about how to teach music but also about how to motivate and inspire students of any age.

Booth, Eric. *The Music Teaching Artist's Bible*. New York, NY: Oxford University Press, 2009.
Practical advice for music teachers from time management to dealing with students.

Hoffer, Charles. *Introduction to Music Education*. Long Grove, IL: Waveland Press, 2009.
Provides a comprehensive, straightforward overview of the field, including its opportunities and its challenges.

Mark, Michael L., and Patrice Madura. *Music Education in Your Hands: An Introduction for Future Teachers*. New York, NY: Routledge, 2010.

Written for future classroom music teachers, this book provides an overview of the music education system.

Peterson, Elizabeth. *The Music Teacher's First Year: Tales of Challenge, Joy and Triumph*. Galesville, MD: Meredith Music Publications, 2011.
A collection of true stories from first-year music teachers.

PERIODICALS

American Music Teacher
Web site: http://www.mtna.org/publications/american-music-teacher
Stay up to date on the latest news and trends in the music field and learn about issues affecting today's music educators

Music Educators Journal
Web site: http://mej.sagepub.com
Published quarterly, *Music Educators Journal* offers peer-reviewed scholarly and practical articles on music teaching approaches and philosophies, instructional techniques, current trends and issues in music education in schools and communities, and the latest in products and services.

Music Teacher Magazine
Web site: http://www.rhinegold.co.uk/magazines
/music_teacher/default.asp?css=1
An international music magazine targeted at school and
private music teachers.

Teaching Music Magazine
Web site: http://musiced.nafme.org/resources
/periodicals/teaching-music-online-edition
Offers practical articles on technology, advocacy resources, and how-to articles about music education.

WEB SITES

Due to the changing nature of Internet links, Rosen Publishing has developed an online list of Web sites related
to the subject of this book. This site is updated regularly.
Please use this link to access the list:

http://www.rosenlinks.com/CCWC/Music

CHAPTER 2

MUSIC CRITIC

Like many writers and journalists, music critics strive to present a fair and accurate representation of the facts, whether they are related to an album or the scoop behind a popular singer or band. Music critics get the information and pass it on. Jobs in music journalism will not make you rich, yet they are relatively glamorous. Competition to meet popular musicians, see their shows, and talk to them about their records, while *getting paid for it* can be intense. If you have the drive to be on the go and the persistence to keep going in a competitive market, this may be a job to look into further.

A DAY IN THE LIFE

The majority of music critics (also called music journalists, music reviewers, and music writers) basically perform a similar task: writing about music in some form. They may work for a local newspaper and write a daily, weekly, or monthly column about what is happening in the music industry. They might also write reviews about concerts, shows, and artists who perform locally. A music critic may also write for Web

New York Times music critic Jon Pareles talks with singer Mary J. Blige. Music critics will often interview artists and bands about their latest albums, tours, or other projects.

sites. As he or she moves from small, local papers to larger newspapers or magazines, a music critic may specialize in a particular style of music, which means he or she may write about rock music or jazz albums.

To get information about the musicians and bands they are writing about, music critics will read background information and past interviews. They will also interview artists and other people in the music business. They may interview a musician in person, over the phone, or via e-mail. If they are reviewing shows, music critics will attend the shows or concerts and then write reviews. They must be able to write well under pressure and finish their reviews shortly after shows. Music critics can't allow their personal preferences to affect reviews; they need to be unbiased and fair.

Music journalists can work full-time or part-time. Sometimes they work as stringers for newspapers or magazines, which means they work each music concert or show as it comes to town. Sometimes music critics work as freelancers, which means they get paid for what they write.

WHAT EDUCATION AND TRAINING DO MUSIC CRITICS NEED?

People who write about music have to be very knowledgeable about all types of music. They must also be good writers. College is not necessary, but it does help greatly; many music journalists who attend college have received degrees in journalism. If you want to be a music critic, you may be able to get a job at a smaller, local newspaper without a college

A great way to train to be a music critic is to join your high school newspaper staff. You will see how newspapers work and get experience writing for a deadline.

degree. To polish your writing skills, you may want to take a writing course, either online, at a local community college, or through a writers' workshop.

To get started as a music critic, you should expect to start at the bottom. It's going to be hard to walk into the offices of *Vibe* or *Spin* and get a job as a writer; experience and longevity are what count. Start training on your own in high school. If your school has a newspaper, see if there are any openings that involve music writing. If your school doesn't offer a paper, try your hand at writing for a local arts paper or newsletter. Look for Web sites that need writers for music reviews and articles. Take any writing jobs you have a chance to during this phase of your development as a writer. This will also give you a sizable portfolio. A portfolio is a résumé, or a listing of your qualifications as a writer—a collection of your work, to use as samples to show prospective editors and employers. Magazines, newspapers, and Web sites don't hire people without an idea of their writing skill and style. You have to start small to build the experience and body of work necessary to work for a major newspaper or music magazine. The idea is to have a collection of clips (published writing samples) to show to a potential employer.

Working on your writing is always a necessity. In addition to classes in school, poke around on the Internet and read what other music critics have written. Almost every site related to music has a section that reviews records and CDs.

Even online music stores post reviews from customers, and that can be a good place to start. Take a look at the major music magazines at the local bookstore or magazine stand, and familiarize yourself with the kinds of records that get reviewed and the way in which they are reviewed. Finally, listen to as much music as you can. If you don't have a good working knowledge of music, you won't be able to succeed as a music critic.

SALARY EXPECTATIONS

The salary of music writers is largely freelance, meaning writers get paid an agreed upon sum of money before they write a piece. The sum is usually paid by the word and can vary. Some magazines and Web sites pay per review. The price per word can be determined by experience. Some writers will take a job for a small sum in the hopes that they will earn more money as they continue to write for and develop a relationship with a particular publication.

CAREER OUTLOOK

Music writing is a very competitive field. As long as people continue to listen to music, they will want to talk about it. If you don't mind starting at the bottom or moving to a place where a music critic is needed, you will have a better chance

of finding work. Just about every town has a newspaper or publication that has a music and entertainment section. Web sites also need music writers.

If you are not writing for anyone and don't have a port-folio or writing samples, write reviews of records you like or feel strongly about, and send them to various publications. Expect not to receive replies to your submissions sometimes, and also be prepared to have your writing rejected. The more you write, the better you'll be, and the better your chances of being published.

Music critics often work under tight deadlines. They may have only a few hours to write a review for a magazine or newspaper after attending a concert.

FOR MORE INFORMATION

ORGANIZATIONS

International Film Music Critic Association (IFMCA)
Web site: http://www.filmmusiccritics.org

Music Critics Association of North America
722 Dulaney Valley Road, #259
Baltimore, MD 21204
(410) 435-3881
Web site: http://www.mcana.org

Society of Professional Journalists
Eugene S. Pulliam National Journalism Center
3909 N. Meridian Street
Indianapolis, IN 46208
(317) 927-8000
Web site: http://www.spj.org

BOOKS

Herbert, Trevor. *Music in Words: A Guide to Researching and Writing About Music*. New York, NY: Oxford University Press, 2009.
A compact guide to researching and writing about music.
Rich, Amanda, and Brittany Rich. *Off the Bus and On the Re-*

cord: *22 Candid Interviews by the Teen Journalists of the Rock Star Stories*. San Francisco, CA: Zest Books, 2009.
This book is a compilation of music interviews by teen music journalists.

Ross, Alex, and Daphne Carr. *Best Music Writing 2011*. Cambridge, MA: De Capo Press, 2011.
An annual title that gathers essays, missives, and musings on every style of music from rock to hip-hop to R & B to jazz to pop to blues.

2013 Writer's Market. Blue Ash, OH: Writer's Digest Books, 2013.
An annual titles for writers of all genres that includes information about outlets that are looking for articles about music.

PERIODICALS

Billboard Magazine
Web site: www.billboard.com
This magazine includes news, analysis, and essential business information about all things music.

MOJO
Web site: http://www.mojo4music.com/blog
MOJO is a British magazine that has some of the best

writing about music on the planet. Go to a bookstore and leaf through a copy; it's like reading the history of rock, R & B, and rap in every issue.

New Musical Express (NME)
Web site: http://www.nme.com
This British magazine is the world's longest running music weekly periodical with writing about newly released music.

Pollstar
Web site: http://www.pollstar.com
A print magazine with an online component, *Pollstar* publishes concert tour schedules for music professionals.

Rolling Stone
Web site: http://www.rollingstone.com
A monthly popular culture magazine covering the entertainment industry, with a special focus on music.

Spin
Web site: http://www.spin.com
The print and online versions of this magazine cover everything you'd want to know about the latest in rock music.

Vibe
Web site: http:// www.vibe.com
Good music writing about the rap and R & B side of music.

WEB SITES

Due to the changing nature of Internet links, Rosen Publishing has developed an online list of Web sites related to the subject of this book. This site is updated regularly. Please use this link to access the list:

http://www.rosenlinks.com/CCWC/Music

CHAPTER 3

WEB SITE CONTENT PRODUCER

Just about everyone has a Web site these days, and if you are a recording artist in the public eye, you'd better have a site that keeps fans informed and interested in your music. If you like music and know your way around a computer and the Internet, you might want to think about a career as a Web site content producer. Content producers are responsible for creating an artist's or record label's Web site and maintaining the site's content.

A DAY IN THE LIFE

Web site content developers help artists design and build a Web site that promotes their music. Web sites give artists a presence on the Web and a place for fans to find information about the band or artist. Web sites are also a place for the latest news, concert dates and information, and new album details. Some music artists use their Web sites to promote and sell albums and other merchandise, including T-shirts.

A Web site content producer will work with an artist to custom design a Web site. Sometimes the designer will update an existing site to add new sections or features.

In addition to just building a Web site, a content manager will also help the artist or band develop a strategic plan for their site. This plan will include what type of information they want to have, how to present it, and how often to update it. A good strategic plan will keep a Web site fresh and innovative, which will keep existing fans coming back and generate buzz that draws in new fans.

Once the site is designed and up and running, the Web site content producer maintains the day-to-day content of the site. He or she makes sure that the content is fresh, informative, user friendly, and interesting. The home page will announce breaking news and other timely information like concert announcements or album news. Content managers may research and write other pages on the site, including artist biographies and profiles, feature stories, interviews, tour and album news, discographies, song lyrics, forums, photos, videos, and more. The Web site content manager may also develop a interactive features such as a blog, a webcast, chats, podcasts, and more that keep the site fresh and exciting. Everything on the site is designed to keep the artist's fans engaged in and involved in the music.

A small emerging artist may need only one content producer. If the artist's site is large and developed, more than one content producer may work on it. In these cases, a senior content producer may oversee the site and supervise other content producers. For large sites, the content producer may be responsible for finding freelance writers to write stories and articles, editing them as needed, and getting them loaded online. He or she may also be responsible for managing staff copywriters, photographers, and graphic artists.

WHAT EDUCATION AND TRAINING DO WEB SITE CONTENT PROVIDERS NEED?

People who build and maintain Web sites needed to be Internet savvy and know HTML. College is not necessary, but it does help greatly. Many Web site content developers who attend college have received degrees in journalism, communications, English, public relations, marketing, music-business management, or liberal arts. If you don't have a college degree, you might want to take a course, workshop, or seminar in public relations, writing, and Web journalism.

Many successful recording artists prefer to hire a Web site content developer with a proven track record. So to get experience, you might work on Web sites for a few new artists to build your portfolio of work. After you've built a reputation and résumé with experience developing, creating, editing, and managing Web content, you will be better able to land a position with a larger band or record label.

Regardless of the size of your client, you'll need to be innovative, creative, and organized as a Web site content developer. If you've got excellent verbal and written communications skills and the ability to juggle multiple projects at the same time, this may be the career for you.

Many recording artists hire a Web site content provider to design a Web site. As the artist announces appearances or records new music, the content provider will update the site to inform fans.

SALARY EXPECTATIONS

Salary for a Web site content developer varies by experience and client. As you gain experience, you can charge more for your work. Some content developers are freelance, working for several small acts at the same time. They may get paid by the hour or receive a set flat fee. Other content producers are employees of the artist or record label, being paid hourly or earning a salary.

CAREER OUTLOOK

The outlook for Web site content producers is fair. They may work for well-known established artists or up-and-coming acts. They may work as freelancers or be employed directly by the recording artist or band, the management company, or the record label. To get started, you might want to look for an internship at a record label, radio station, or local newspaper where you can get experience writing and making contacts. If you hear of an up-and-coming band, volunteer to design their Web site for free. If you do a good job, you can use them as a reference to land a paying client. Regularly check for openings on music industry career sites, artist Web sites, or local music trade publications.

FOR MORE INFORMATION

ORGANIZATIONS

International Association of Internet Professionals
Web site: http://internetprofessionals.org
This nonprofit, global organization provides an informational and social hub for Internet professionals with expertise in mobile, social, analytics, search, and emerging technologies.

International Webmasters Association (IWA)
119 E. Union Street, Suite #A
Pasadena, CA 91103
(626) 449-3709
Web site: http://www.iwanet.org
IWA is a nonprofit professional association that provides educational and certification standards for Web professionals.

The National Academy of Recording Arts & Sciences (NARAS)
3030 Olympic Boulevard
Santa Monica, CA 90404
(310) 392-3777
Web site: http://www.grammy.org

An organization of musicians, producers, recording engineers, and other recording professionals including Web site content developers dedicated to improving the quality of life and cultural condition for music and its makers.

The World Organization of Webmasters
P.O. Box 1743
Folsom, CA 95630
(916) 989-2933
Web site: http://webprofessionals.org/about
The World Organization of Webmasters is a nonprofit professional association dedicated to the support of individuals and organizations who create, manage, or market Web sites.

BOOKS

Crowder, David A. *Building a Web Site for Dummies*. Hoboken, NJ: Wiley, 2010.
Straightforward info on how to build a Web site, even for beginners.

Hoole, Gavin, and Cheryl Smith. *The Really, Really, Really, Easy Step-by-Step Guide to Building Your Own Website: For Absolute Beginners of All Ages*. London, UK: New Holland, 2008.

This step-by-step practical guide helps users create a site from scratch, from planning the structure and registering the domain to attracting visitors and updating content.

MacDonald, Matthew. *Creating a Website: The Missing Manual*. Sebastopol, CA: O'Reilly Media, 2011.
This Missing Manual gives you all the tools, techniques, and expert advice you need to build a Web site.

Selfridge, Benjamin, Peter Selfridge, and Jennifer Osburn. *A Teen's Guide to Creating Web Pages and Blogs*. Waco, TX: Prufrock Press, 2009.
Geared toward teens, this guide shows how to publish exciting Web pages and blogs.

PERIODICALS

A List Apart
Web site: http://alistapart.com
An online magazine with articles and analysis for code, content, and Web design.

Smashing Magazine
Web site: http://www.smashingmagazine.com
An online magazine for professional Web designers and

developers, with a focus on useful techniques, best practices, and valuable information.

Web Designer
Web site: http://www.webdesignermag.co.uk/
This UK publication has a tutorial-based format that follows projects in Dreamweaver, Flash, and Photoshop.

WEB SITES

Due to the changing nature of Internet links, Rosen Publishing has developed an online list of Web sites related to the subject of this book. This site is updated regularly. Please use this link to access the list:

http://www.rosenlinks.com/CCWC/Music

CHAPTER 4

RECORDING ENGINEER

Recording engineers (also called audio engineers or sound technicians) can perform a wide range of jobs. They deal with the processing of live and recorded sound, which covers a large number of employment possibilities and can also lead to other related job opportunities in the music industry.

A DAY IN THE LIFE

Simply put, recording engineers make things sound good. Recording engineers process sound; that is, they work with sound that comes through microphones or amplifiers or other sources and adjust the levels of the various sounds (the bass, drums, voice, and guitar of a band, for instance) and make them work together as a whole listening experience. Recording engineers are often called soundmen or sound-women because sound is the focus point of their field.

Recording engineers adjust the sounds of live and recorded performances to ensure that everyone can hear what's being said or played and that the sound is as free of disturbances as possible. Disturbances refer to anything that interferes with sound quality; one good example is feedback, which is the high-pitched sound that you may hear when someone talks

A recording engineer works at an audio control panel to adjust sound. The engineer makes sure that whether the music is live or recorded, everyone can hear what is being played.

into a microphone. Recording engineers also think about how sound will travel in a particular place, and they know exactly where to put microphones or equipment to ensure maximum sound quality. If you look on the back of a CD or album, the person who is credited as the "engineer" is actually a recording engineer. The producers of recorded music often have recording engineer training, as well.

A tool many recording engineers work with is called a mixing board, which is a more advanced version of the mixer that a DJ at a small- to mid-sized event may use. Almost any public event—political speeches, television broadcasts, live concerts—requires the services of an recording engineer.

Recording engineers are also able to perform a great number of sound-related jobs. In addition to figuring out and monitoring sound requirements, they can also repair and service sound equipment. This can range from microphones to turntables to public address systems. Some areas of the field involve the installation of sound systems at local clubs, arenas, and radio stations. Some sound technicians work in motion pictures and commercials, inserting necessary sound effects to enhance a program.

For larger or more complicated jobs, recording engineers often have assistants who help them with some of the details of a job; checking cables and connections for the sound at a stadium would be too much for one person to keep track of, for instance. Some people who have trained as recording engineers may start out helping someone in a very specific manner on their way to greater responsibilities.

WHAT EDUCATION AND TRAINING DO RECORDING ENGINEERS NEED?

Both education and training are necessary to be an effective and employable recording engineer. Some colleges offer sound engineering programs; however, a college degree is not necessary to be a recording engineer. There are a few different pipelines to success or qualification.

SALARY EXPECTATIONS

Many soundmen and soundwomen who work at clubs and venues are paid on a per-night basis and can use this

MIXING CONSOLES

A mixing console, or mixing board, is the most important tool used by recording engineers. Indoors and out, mixing boards allow the audience to hear a proper balance of all of the performers. Every microphone used in a performance is plugged into the sound person's console. The board is really like a sound laboratory; all voices and sounds come together and are processed by the mixing board (this is what "mixing" is). Every mixing board has a series of channels, which allow focus to be placed on different aspects of a performance. Let's say a mixing board has sixteen channels. One of those channels may be devoted just to the bass guitar. This allows a recording engineer to adjust the bass guitar's level before it goes to the speaker to prevent it from being too loud and drowning out other instruments or from being too quiet and unheard by an audience. Imagine fifteen more items filling the remaining channels— that's the raw material of the soundman's job during a performance. Using a mixing board allows sound personnel to adjust bass, treble ,and midrange and to also use electronic effects to enhance specific aspects of a performance, while allowing the rest of the band or group or orchestra to play on.

experience to obtain a full-time job as a recording engineer on television or radio. With time in the business and more responsibility, audio engineers at very high levels can demand higher salaries.

A recording engineer often works with a mixing console. Adjusting the controls, the engineer makes sure that the audience hears the proper balance of performers and instruments.

CAREER OUTLOOK

The outlook is good, thanks to the fact that there are many segments of the entertainment industry that rely on sound technicians. Freelance work can also be a good way to make steady or extra income; fill-in work for last-minute replacements can be high. In addition to music, someone with a recording engineering background will be able to find work in a variety of connected fields, such as special audio effects for motion pictures and music video sound.

ADDITIONAL INFORMATION

Recording engineers frequently work long hours. The person in charge of sound for a concert can't arrive with the audience; he or she has to be at the venue hours early to check sound levels for various equipment. Many events that involve audio are often at night or outside; this enables people in this field to sometimes work second jobs or pursue other employment interests. The field of recording engineering relies more and more on technology; an ability to understand computers or a willingness to learn is a great help. Lastly, recording engineers are in the spotlight, especially if there is a sound problem, which can make for a stressful environment occasionally.

FOR MORE INFORMATION

ORGANIZATIONS
Audio Engineering Society (AES)
60 East 42nd Street, Room 2520
New York, NY 10165-2520
(212) 661-8528
Web site: http://www.aes.org

Institute of Professional Sound (IPS)
P.O. Box 208
Havant
Hampshire PO9 9BQ
United Kingdom
Web site: http://www.ips.org.uk

Recording Industry Association of America (RIAA)
1025 F Street NW, 10th Floor
Washington, DC 20004
(202) 775-0101
Web site: http://www.riaa.com

BOOKS
Dittmar, Tim. *Audio Engineering 101: A Beginner's Guide
   to Music Production*. Waltham, MA: Focal, 2012.
This is a beginner's guide to audio engineering.

Izhaki, Roey. *Mixing Audio: Concepts, Practices and Tools*. Boston, MA: Focal, 2012.
Covers the entire process of mixing audio, from fundamental concepts to advanced techniques, and offers many audio samples, tips, and tricks.

Owsinski, Bobby. *The Mixing Engineer's Handbook*. Clifton Park, NY: Delmar, 2013.
Points out the key elements of mixing for beginners.

While, Ira. *Audio Made Easy (Or How to Be a Sound Engineer Without Really Trying)*. Milwaukee, WI: Hal Leonard Publishing Corporation, 2007.
An introduction to live audio and recording written by a professional recording engineer.

PERIODICALS

Audio Media
Web site: http://www.audiomedia.com
Bills itself as the world's leading professional audio technology magazine.

Electronic Musician
Web site: http://www.emusician.com
Trade journal for serious recording professionals.

Mix
Web site: http://mixonline.com/
Trade magazine for those interested in commercial and
 project studio recording.

Professional Sound
Web site: http://www.professional-sound.com
A bimonthly trade journal for the professional sound
 engineer.

WEB SITES
Due to the changing nature of Internet links, Rosen Publishing has developed an online list of Web sites related
to the subject of this book. This site is updated regularly.
Please use this link to access the list:

http://www.rosenlinks.com/CCWC/Music

CHAPTER 5

MUSICIAN

Playing music can be a profession you pursue. There are some important factors to consider, however, and we'll look at a few of them in the next few paragraphs. If you don't know how to play an instrument or sing, this may not be the profession for you. Years of practice and dedication are necessary before a person can perform at the level of a professional musician.

A DAY IN THE LIFE

If you play an instrument, your services will probably fall into one of two categories: session musician or general business musician. Session musicians (also called session players, sidemen and sidewomen, or backup musicians) work in studios or onstage and are given a piece of music to learn and play according to the instructions of the bandleader or producer of a recording session or concert. Session musicians are highly skilled and need to know how to read music and most likely write or transcribe music notation, which is the written language musicians everywhere use. Most session musicians

Some musicians join together to form a band. The band's musicians may play live concerts in many type of venues, including local clubs, restaurants, festivals, or arenas.

specialize in one instrument or one type of instrument, such as stringed instruments or woodwinds, but playing more than one instrument can make you more valuable and enable you to find work more often. Many session musicians don't perform onstage; they play their instruments on movie and television sound tracks and music for commercials, in addition to music for bands. Some session musicians are members of orchestras that play classical music. A seat on an orchestra pays very well, and competition can be fierce. Session musicians need to be easygoing and able to adapt to a new situation quickly because they are often given music that they have never seen before and need to play it in a short time.

Some professional musicians are known as general musicians. These musicians have learned a variety of songs, usually popular songs, written by someone else, from many periods of popular music. This is called their repertoire. A repertoire is like a music résumé; general musicians use their repertoire to obtain work at a variety of situations. General musicians can work alone or with a regular group of

Several musicians in a rock band, including a vocalist, guitar players, a drummer, and a keyboard player, gather to rehearse new music in a studio before an upcoming performance.

musicians and play events such as weddings, birthday parties, and corporate functions.

A musician can also rely on his or her voice as an instrument. Professional singers' voices have many classifications that are organized by vocal range, which includes soprano, contralto, tenor, and baritone, or by style of music. People who sing professionally also need to be able to read music; the human voice is an instrument that requires as much training as, say, a cello.

WHAT EDUCATION AND TRAINING DO MUSICIANS NEED?

You don't need music school to be a musician, but some training is definitely required to work professionally. If you have some experience, the first step you may want to take is to join the band at your school or in your community, or take private lessons outside of school. If you want to sing, join the choir or audition for a school play or musical. If your school doesn't offer these activities, you may want to look outside the academic world and in the direction of semiprofessional performance, such as summer stock plays or smaller, independent productions.

If you don't go to college, it may be a good idea to take a few classes in some important areas of music. Most music

A jazz musician performs in a New Orleans nightclub. Many musicians enjoy performing in front of a live audience, in small clubs or large arenas.

that's played today has roots in classical music—that could be a good place to start. Remember, the later you start, the more difficult the path to success may be.

SALARY EXPECTATIONS

The average salary for musicians and singers can vary widely. There are plenty of things that factor into what you can make as a musician, including your résumé (where you've worked before), reputation, and hours. Some musicians work as session musicians and general musicians at the same time. Doing multiple jobs at the same time can definitely increase what you will make. Many musicians teach privately to supplement their income. The smaller the orchestra and the region, the fewer number of performances—this means a lower salary.

The average musician doesn't strike it rich. People who play music professionally do it because they love what they do. There is often downtime in between jobs for musicians, and many encounter unemployment while waiting for the next job.

CAREER OUTLOOK

As we said earlier, the environment for musicians is highly competitive. Many aspects of the music business are very attractive; performing as a musician to crowds and playing with other talented musicians falls into the same category. If this is the route you choose, make yourself as marketable as possible. Learn additional instruments, and most of all, *practice*. People like live music, and as long as they do, professional musicians will be needed.

ADDITIONAL INFORMATION

Most musicians work odd hours, which means late nights and weekends; these are the times when most people choose to seek out entertainment. This is another job that requires you to be a "people person." Musicians have to know how to get along with other people, both in bands they may play with, as well as with an audience. Shy people may want to reconsider a career as a professional musician. Geography makes a difference, too. It's easier to find work as a session musician, for instance, if you live in or near a city that has more recording facilities than a small town may. New York, Nashville, and Los Angeles may provide you with more opportunities to audition and find work than smaller towns will.

FOR MORE INFORMATION

ORGANIZATIONS

American Federation of Musicians
1501 Broadway, Suite 600
New York, NY 10036
(212) 869-1330
Web site: http://www.afm.org

Country Music Association (CMA)
One Music Circle South
Nashville, TN 37203
(615) 244-2840
Web site: http://www.cmaworld.com

Creative Musicians Coalition
P.O. Box 6205
Peoria, IL 61601-6205
(309) 685-4843
Web site: http://www.aimcmc.com

Music and Entertainers Industry Educators Association
  (MEISA)
Web site: http://www.meiea.org/about.html

BOOKS

Aretha, David. *Awesome African-American Rock and Soul Musicians*. Berkeley Heights, NJ: Enslow, 2013.
Biographies of several legendary rock and soul musicians.

Cartlidge, Cherese. *Beyoncé*. Detroit, MI: Lucent, 2012.
Biography of the legendary singer.

Goodmark, Robyn, and Adrienne Yan. *Girls Rock: How to Get Your Group Together and Make Some Noise*. New York, NY: Billboard, 2008.
Tips and advice on how to put together a girl band.

Nathan, Amy. *The Young Musician's Survival Guide: Tips from Teens and Pros*. New York, NY: Oxford University Press, 2008.
Information and advice for teen musicians.

PERIODICALS

Bass Player
Web site: http://www.bassplayer.com
A popular magazine for bassists.

Billboard
Web site: http://www.billboard.com
One of the oldest trade magazines for musicians and
    the music industry.

Guitar Player
Web site: http://www.guitarplayer.com
A popular magazine for guitarists

Performer Magazine
Web site: http://performermag.com
Performer Magazine is an American music magazine
    aimed at independent musicians.

WEB SITES
Due to the changing nature of Internet links, Rosen Publishing has developed an online list of Web sites related
to the subject of this book. This site is updated regularly.
Please use this link to access the list:

http://www.rosenlinks.com/CCWC/Music

CHAPTER 6

INSTRUMENT RESTORATION AND REPAIR

Musicians play the instruments, but who keeps them running and sounding good? What if a piano is out of tune? What does a violinist do if his or her violin is broken? What does a trumpeter do with a dented horn? They all call on instrument restorers and repairers.

A DAY IN THE LIFE

Music repair and restoration requires a greater deal of skill than many of the jobs described in this book. People who perform this work also usually develop a large amount of knowledge about a particular type of instrument, rather than attempt to repair every type of instrument under the sun. People who want their pianos tuned don't call tuba repair people—they call the expert on pianos.

There are four major types of instruments that people repair: Piano/Organ, Band, Violins, and Guitars. Although guitars and violins both have strings, they are different in

A violin maker repairs a cello in her workshop. She works carefully with the wood and strings to restore and repair any damage to the instrument.

many other ways. Therefore, special attention is needed for each musical instrument.

Piano and organ repairers and restorers have to deal with the thousands (that's correct, *thousands*) of parts that make up the average piano if keys stick or do not move when pressed. If you were to look inside a piano, you would notice dozens of strings. To tune a piano, each string has to be adjusted individually—this usually takes about two hours on the average.

Band instruments are those instruments played by traditional orchestras, rather than those used by a rock band with guitars and amplifiers. Band instruments include brass and wind instruments, as well as percussion instruments. Brass and wind instruments are blown through, and include tubas, trumpets, trombones, oboes, cornets, French horns, flugelhorns, saxophones, contrabassoons, and…

the list could go on for a long time. These people adjust and repair some of these instruments. In order to know what's wrong with an instrument, a repairer needs to know how to play that instrument. Repairers and restorers also perform the important task of cleaning musical equipment. Brass and wind instruments have many moving parts that could stick or not allow air to pass through them correctly if dirt and dust were to accumulate over a long time.

Percussion instruments are instruments that have skin stretched over a frame and are hit to make sounds: snare drums, congas, tympani, and bongos all fall into this category. Repair persons may have to cut and stretch a new skin over a snare drum or adjust its tension, or repair cracks in cymbals.

Violin restorers tune and repair violins and other stringed instruments that are played with a bow, such as cellos and violas (larger violins with a deeper sound). Guitar tuners and repairers do the same thing to electric and acoustic guitars, as well as to bass guitars and other variations on non-bowed string instruments. In addition to the main categories, there are other instruments that require special and singular attention, such as pipe organs, electronic organs, and electronic keyboards.

Musical instrument repairers and restorers often work alone and in a relatively quiet environment in order to tune instruments as well as they possibly can. This type of work is not recommended for those who like to be on the go and meet people during the course of a workday. Restorers and repairers can work in a variety of locales, including repair shops and music stores. Piano tuners often have to travel to do their work, since the instruments are difficult to move.

WHAT EDUCATION AND TRAINING DO REPAIRERS AND RESTORERS NEED?

This is one line of work that requires extensive training, and it must be hands-on. Most places that hire restorers and repairers prefer schooling of some sort for their employees. Many community colleges and music schools offer coursework in instrument repair and restoration for the categories mentioned earlier. Instrument repair schools offer specific training and require one or two years of study.

Without schooling, it is still possible to succeed as a repairer or restorer. The way to do this is through an apprenticeship, which is a more professional version of an internship. The key is to start now if this is a career you're considering. The number of repairers and restorers who take on assistants or apprentices is very low, and the later you start, the tougher it's going to be. There are still a few places that do offer on-the-job instruction to trainees. Usually, trainees perform another task while

Students in Brazil take a class to learn how to repair guitars. After the students have repaired the damaged instruments, they will be donated to local children.

they learn a trade. For example, a trainee at a musical instrument store might sell sheet music or stock inventory while he or she is learning the ropes of repair with an expert. On the average, training in this way can take anywhere from two to five years. Interested? Start soon!

SALARY EXPECTATIONS

For experienced professionals, salaries can be quite high. Of course, the salary amount depends on the specialist's experience level and where he or she is working. If an instrument is rare or difficult to repair, the specialist can earn more.

CAREER OUTLOOK

If you are interested in repair and restoration, you should try to get involved at an early age if you feel like this is an avenue of employment that you may want to pursue. Since training takes some time, job openings come and go at a slower rate than in other professions. The more training a person has will make him or her all the more valuable in the next few years.

Recent surveys have indicated that there is a shortage of trained, competent instrument repair technicians. This shortage will increase as many older technicians enter their retirement years. As a result, demand for technicians is projected to be high for several years.

FOR MORE INFORMATION

ORGANIZATIONS

Acoustical Society of America
Suite 1NO1 2 Huntington Quadrangle
Melville, NY 11747-4502
(516) 576-2360
Web site: http://acousticalsociety.org

Musical Instrument Technicians Association (MITA)
Web site: http://www.mitatechs.com

National Association of Professional Band Instrument
Repair Technicians (NAPBIRT)
P.O. Box 51
Normal, IL 61761
(309) 452-4257
Web site: http://www.napbirt.org

Piano Technicians Guild (PTG)
4444 Forest Avenue
Kansas City, KS 66106
(913) 432-9975
Web site: http://www.ptg.org

BOOKS

Atria, Michael. *Violin Repair Guide*. New York, NY: Hal Leonard Corporation. 2004.
This guide provides illustrated step-by-step instructions for bow rehairing, repair, and restoration of the violin, viola, cello, and string bass.

Erlewine, Dan. *The Guitar Player Repair Guide*. New York, NY: Backbeat Books, 2007.
This book, for beginners to experts, is a step-by-step manual to maintaining and repairing electric and acoustic guitars and basses.

Pagliaro, Michael. *The Musical Instrument Desk Reference: A Guide to How Band and Orchestral Instruments Work*. Lanham, MD: Scarecrow Press, 2012.
A quick, visually rich reference guide to band and orchestral instruments.

Rubin, Dave, and Doug Redler. *Guitarist's Guide to Maintenance and Repair*. New York, NY: Hal Leonard Corporation, 2012.
Written by a guitar tech, this book covers tips to keep guitars and amps healthy.

PERIODICALS

The Journal of Musical Instrument Technology
Web site: http://www.musictrader.com/mitindex.html
This publication is written for people who have an interest
   in the repair, build, or design of musical instruments.

WEB SITES

Due to the changing nature of Internet links, Rosen Publishing has developed an online list of Web sites related
to the subject of this book. This site is updated regularly.
Please use this link to access the list:

http://www.rosenlinks.com/CCWC/Music

CHAPTER 7

RADIO STATION EMPLOYEE

Music broadcasters, simply put, work together to create the programs you hear on the radio. The effort of many people collaborating, or working together, is absolutely necessary to make sure that music gets from the artist to the general public. Thanks to technology, there are many opportunities to work in music broadcasting, such as the radio and Internet stations.

Disc jockeys are the people whose voices represent a station. They sometimes are known as radio personalities or announcers. DJs can introduce news, weather, and most important to us, music. Unfortunately, most DJs on the air don't get to pick what they want to play. Instead, they are usually given a playlist by programming directors, who decide what a station is going to play, based on the station's format, or music type. How many formats are there? Turn on a radio and turn the dial—every type of music is represented, from country to rock to rap to dance. Some smaller radio stations and Internet music sites are free-form, which means they may not play only one sort of music. These are great places to work if you want to learn about a large range of music types.

Music directors are in charge of keeping a station's music catalog, or library, up-to-date as new recordings are released by record companies. The playlist of a station is always changing, which can be both exciting and frustrating at the same time. Every week, the programming director and music director (sometimes it's the same person) decide which songs to drop or add from the station's playlist.

Guess what? Radio stations also need sound engineers. People who listen to the radio want what they hear to sound good, just like concertgoers or people who want to see a Broadway show or buy a new record. Luckily, many parts of the music business are so related that with experience and training, people can do many jobs at once or move from one area to another. It takes more than one engineer to make a station run. Often, a few sound engineers will work for the chief engineer of a station, who is responsible for all of the technical aspects of a broadcast, to make sure sounds travel from the microphone to the radio speaker to our ears.

The jobs that are available in music broadcasting touch on many aspects of a business. Radio stations also need people to write material for the DJs to say, maintain the station's electronic equipment, and to sell advertising time to businesses that want to promote their companies.

A DJ performs at a local event. Many radio station DJs are local celebrities and will appear at events around town to promote the radio station.

WHAT EDUCATION AND TRAINING DO RADIO STATION EMPLOYEES NEED?

Although colleges offer broadcasting degrees, you can still gain entry into the world of broadcasting without one; however, it will be more difficult to do so. People with computer skills are at an advantage here; more and more radio outfits are becoming increasingly digital and computerized. Take advantage of computer programs your school may have. After school, you may want to invest in some basic broadcasting courses at a local college to get a better understanding of the technical side of the industry. There are also broadcasting schools that offer one- or two-year programs in all aspects of the business.

Without a bachelor's degree in broadcasting, it is a little more

Radio station DJs talk and play music on the air. Some radio station employees start in other positions and work their way up to an on-air announcing job.

difficult to break into the announcing side of radio. Experience is as important as a college degree in some aspects of the radio business. Try to obtain as much as possible while you're still in school. If you want to be an on-air personality, get involved in activities at your school that are related: the debate team or a school play, or announcing for the football or basketball team.

Some radio stations at colleges and small local stations need volunteers or interns to help out in the off months. This is free training. Use this opportunity to get involved early; it will pay off, even if you don't get a paycheck for the time you spend learning part of the trade. The more motivation you display as an intern may make the difference between being hired or not for a paying job down the road.

SALARY EXPECTATIONS

If you're interning to gain on-the-job training, there is no pay; this is definitely a profession that requires experience before you can rely on it as a steady source of income. For paid employees, salaries vary, depending on the particular job a person does. Popular music personalities make more money, but to reach that level takes a little time. Salaries for behind-the-scenes people like technicians vary according to time in a position and experience.

CAREER OUTLOOK

Employment prospects are fair, depending on the size of the market and radio station. In smaller markets, there is often large turnover because of low pay. Jobs open as people move up to higher paying positions in larger markets and stations. Small market radio stations allow for disc jockeys to advance to the position of program director or music director. With experience, you can also look for a position at a larger station in a bigger city.

FOR MORE INFORMATION

ORGANIZATIONS

American Federation of Television and Radio Artists
  (SAG-AFTRA)
5757 Wilshire Boulevard, 7th Floor
Los Angeles, CA 90036-3600
(323) 634-8100
(855) 724-2387
Web site: http://www.sagaftra.org

Country Radio Broadcasters
819 18th Avenue South
Nashville, TN 37203
(615) 327-4487

National Association of Broadcast Employees & Technicians (NABET)
501 3rd Street NW
Washington, DC 20001
(202) 434-1254
Web site: http://www.nabetcwa.org

National Association of Broadcasters (NAB)
1771 N Street NW

Washington, DC 20036
(202) 429-5300
Web site: http://www.nab.org

BOOKS

Keith, Michael. *The Radio Station: Broadcast, Satellite, and Internet*. Burlington, MA: Focal Press, 2010.
This book details all departments within a radio station, be it a terrestrial, satellite, or Internet operation, from the inside out, covering technology to operations, and sales to syndication.

Miller, Carol. *Up All Night: My Life and Times in Rock Radio*. New York, NY: HarperCollins, 2012.
Memoir by American rock 'n' roll disc jockey Carol Miller.

Schneider, Chris. *Starting Your Career in Broadcasting: Working On and Off the Air in Radio and Television*. New York, NY: Allworth Press, 2007.
A complete guide to starting in radio; includes advice from top radio personalities.

Stamz, Richard, and Patrick Roberts. *Give 'Em Soul, Richard!: Race, Radio, and Rhythm and Blues in Chicago*. Champaign, IL: University of Illinois Press, 2010.
Stamz, a major radio personality in Chicago in the

1950s, helped to establish the black radio market and provide broader airing of rhythm and blues music.

PERIODICALS

Radio Ink

Web site: http://www.radioink.com

Radio Ink is a radio-industry trade publication for the radio broadcasting industry. Its mission is to provide relevant management information, tips, and ideas for those operating radio stations.

WEB SITES

Due to the changing nature of Internet links, Rosen Publishing has developed an online list of Web sites related to the subject of this book. This site is updated regularly. Please use this link to access the list:

http://www.rosenlinks.com/CCWC/Music

CHAPTER 8

MUSIC PUBLICIST

One way to stay connected to music is to help spread the word about it. If you like to talk about who's who in music and what they're doing, you can turn this desire into another employment option. The average person doesn't have the opportunity to keep up-to-date on every single record or CD coming out every week on the hundreds of record labels that exist in the United States and Europe and other parts of the world. This is where a music publicist steps in.

A DAY IN THE LIFE

A publicist or press agent works with record labels, management, and artists to increase public knowledge of a particular song, record, album, or musician. The key word in this line of work is publicity. People who work in publicity are mostly concerned with making their client or project as public and well known as possible.

On a day-to-day basis, a publicist must be able to write press releases and assemble press kits that include the artist's biography, pictures, reprints of past articles and reviews—all of which are given to music editors, disc jockeys, and other

Country singer Carrie Underwood poses for a picture with record executives, radio station employees, and her publicist. Underwood's publicist is responsible for coordinating the singer's promotional appearances.

to spread the word about the artist. Sometimes, a publicist will also put together a press conference and make sure to get the right people to attend and cover the event. Publicists create hype for an artist. They attend parties, luncheons, and dinners on a client's behalf, talk incessantly about their client, and make contacts in the industry.

INTERVIEW: SEVEN QUESTIONS WITH A FAN RELATIONS SPECIALIST,

Candace Orlandi, Love and Theft, Pittsburgh, Pennsylvania

1. HOW DID YOU GET INVOLVED WITH PROMOTING MUSIC TO THE FANS? I was working as a DJ for a local radio station and got interested in this new band. I messaged them about writing an article about them for a magazine and kept in touch. Later when their label closed down, I offered to help out with fan relations.

2. WHAT EXACTLY DO YOU DO AS A FAN RELATIONS SPECIALIST? I do a lot of social media management, updating the band's Facebook page, sending out tweets. I also come up with ideas for promotions, contests, and giveaways to get the fans excited.

3. HAD YOU EVER DONE ANYTHING LIKE THIS BEFORE? No! I'd never done anything like this. I was a huge music fan myself, and I knew what I wanted as a fan from an artist. Plus, working at the radio station I think helped me know the music industry, and I made connections through radio.

4. WHAT'S THE BEST PART OF YOUR JOB? For me, it's connecting with people. I love seeing people, like fans who drive hours to a meet and greet. Seeing their reactions is great. I know that feeling, I still geek out over bands I love!

5. WHAT'S THE WORST PART OF THE JOB? Stress! There's a lot of stress dealing with everything. People expect a lot and so much is on your shoulders it can get overwhelming at times. Definitely there can be a lot of pressure.

6. HOW HAS THE INTERNET CHANGED THE MUSIC INDUSTRY AND PROMOTION? Social media is great! It puts things into the hands of the individual person. For bands and fans, everything is in their hands now, not stuck at a record label.

7. DO YOU LIKE YOUR JOB? Love it!

A publicist may have an assistant who helps with tasks. Assistant publicists often go with an artist to publicity appearances such as radio interviews, television spots, or general public events. They will also go with the artist to photo shoots and interviews. Like his or her boss, an assistant publicist might attend dinners, luncheons, and other parties on behalf of a client or company. As a result, people in these jobs often work late hours.

The Internet is ideal for promotions. For every person who lives in a city or urban area, there is someone in a smaller town who may not have immediate access to entertainment; however, many people either own a computer or have access to one with Internet capabilities. Publicists use the Internet and e-mail to inform people of upcoming tours, recordings, and general news involving their clients.

On a larger scale, bigger publicity companies may work directly with a record label or management company to develop a general marketing strategy to get word to the public about a musical act. Bigger labels have more money to use to promote their artists, which makes it easier to get the word out than, for instance, a local artist who may not have the resources to take out television and radio ads to promote himself or herself.

Music publicists use unique or memorable items and events to make both their client and their client's music more memorable. They may organize

Singers in the British group One Direction autograph copies of their CD for a promotional event to generate publicity for the band.

giveaways, contests, and meet and greets where fans can interact directly with the artist.

To be successful, a music publicist must be able to work under pressure. There are constant deadlines in this career, along with ever-changing projects, tasks, and clients. A good publicist can work with any type of client and find a creative way to market the client to the press and listeners.

WHAT EDUCATION AND TRAINING DO MUSIC PUBLICISTS NEED?

As with most jobs in the music business, there aren't any programs that specifically teach music publicity. However, many community colleges offer basic marketing courses, which provide solid backgrounds

Music publicists can learn the basics of publicity and promotion in marketing classes. Communication classes and workshops can teach skills that are helpful for music publicists.

in the principles behind publicity and promotion. Courses in communications also give you basic skills that you will use as a publicist. One way to become a part of this side of the music business is to intern part-time to gain some knowledge about the general goings-on until a paid position opens up. Many people who work in publicity have formerly worked at record labels or other music industry jobs and have learned a little about publicity that way. Some people even decide to branch out and start their own publicity companies after they have learned the basics from a larger company.

SALARY EXPECTATIONS

Record companies generally have a number of publicists on staff. Publicists can also find work in firms that specialize in music business publicity or public relations, along with jobs at radio stations, concert halls, clubs, arenas, and music stores. Salary depends on the company and its size. A company with many clients will pay more but will probably require you to work longer hours, and the pressure could be much greater than at a smaller firm. Part of your salary may also depend on your personal ability to attract and produce results for certain clients.

Some publicists work independently, where they gain their own clients and are paid a fee based on each job instead of a salary. Clients pay independent publicists a wide range of fees, depending on the size of the client, the amount of work required, and the experience of the publicist.

CAREER OUTLOOK

As long as musicians and bands want to attract listeners, they will most likely need assistance in making that a reality. The music business is constantly changing, so the outlook is fair to good. Again, it is usually easy to obtain an internship but more difficult to be taken on by any company as a part- or full-time employee.

FOR MORE INFORMATION

ORGANIZATIONS

American Association of Independent Music
132 Delancey Street, 2nd Floor
New York, NY 10002
Web site: http://a2im.org

American Marketing Association
311 S. Wacker Drive, Suite 5800
Chicago, IL 60606
(800) AMA-1150 (262-1150)
Web site: http://www.marketingpower.com

Association of Theatrical Press Agents and Managers
    (ATPAM)
62 W 45th Street, Suite 901
New York, NY 10036
(212) 719-3666
Web site: http://www.atpam.com

Public Relations Society of America
33 Maiden Lane, Floor 11
New York, NY 10038

(212) 460-1400
Web site: http://www.prsa.org

BOOKS

King, Mike. *Music Marketing: Press, Promotion, Distribution and Retail*. Boston, MA: Berklee Press, 2009.
A Berklee expert discusses how to market and distribute songs and artists, with the most effective marketing strategies and digital technologies.

Lathrop, Tad. *This Business of Music Marketing & Promotion*. New York, NY: Billboard Books, 2005.
This book details promotional skills, publicity plans, royalty guidelines, and more to create a successful music marketing plan.

Miller, Michael. *The Complete Idiot's Guide to the Music Business*. New York, NY: Alpha Books, 2010.
A solid overview of the music business, including chapters on promotions, merchandising, and online publicity.

Passman, Donald. *All You Need to Know About the Music Business*. New York, NY: Simon & Schuster, 2012.

Advice on creating, selling, sharing, and protecting music in the digital age.

PERIODICALS

One Way Magazine
Web site: http://www.onewaymagazine.com
A print and online magazine that is a music promotion and marketing tool targeted to adult music fans, showcasing a wide variety of music genres.

Vents Magazine
Web site: http://www.ventsmagazine.com
An online music and entertainment magazine created to spread the word about little-known bands.

WEB SITES

Due to the changing nature of Internet links, Rosen Publishing has developed an online list of Web sites related to the subject of this book. This site is updated regularly. Please use this link to access the list:

http://www.rosenlinks.com/CCWC/Music

CHAPTER 9

INDEPENDENT DISC JOCKEY

Playing music for the general public is not just reserved for radio personalities anymore. If you have a good-sized collection of music, you may want to try your hand at playing music for income. No matter what the name or how it happens to be spelled—deejay, DJ, disc jockey—this is yet another way to make music part of your employment future.

A DAY IN THE LIFE

Depending on the type of music and venue you are interested in, the setting of your job may vary. Performing as a DJ can take you from playing music at local events like parties all the way to traveling and deejaying for hundreds or even thousands of people. Some DJs only perform to supplement their income; some work so often that they need managers and booking agents to keep track of their busy schedules. Both ends of the spectrum can be entertaining, rewarding, and lucrative.

The first step to becoming a DJ is to obtain equipment. Depending on how much equipment you need, prices may vary but you may not want to spend a large amount of money in the early stages, at least until you decide whether or not

deejaying is for you. The equipment needs to be portable because at larger venues, DJs are usually expected to arrive with their own equipment and connect it to a sound system provided by the establishment that hires them. You need to have two turntables or decks to play music and some sort of mixer to mix the sounds from the two decks. If your venue does not have its own sound system, you'll have to bring some sort of portable speakers to amplify the music. You'll also need a microphone for talking to your audience and introducing songs, as well as a pair of headphones so that you can listen to music that you are getting ready while another song is playing.

DJs use different techniques when playing music. They cut or cue up duplicate copies of the same record in order to play the same passage back and forth. DJs scratch by moving a vinyl record back and forth on a turntable, and they beatmatch by matching up the beats of two different songs.

As an independent DJ, you can work in a variety of venues and locations. Club DJs play their music at parties, local clubs, and other events. If things go well (meaning people come to hear you and want to keep coming back) you may be rewarded with a residency. In short, a residency is a performance slot on a regular basis. Residencies are usually weekly or monthly, and they are good goals to reach for.

People also hire DJs to work at specialty events such as weddings, birthday parties, and other sorts of celebrations.

An independent disc jockey travels to a variety of venues to work. His or her equipment must be portable and easily set up in many different conditions.

You also need to be flexible because people who hold and schedule these events usually have a specific idea of the type of music they would like their guests to hear. Events like these are good ways to promote yourself; word of mouth can bring several new customers, and you could find yourself performing for many of the satisfied guests at *their* own celebrations.

One initial drawback to deejaying may be age. Many places that hire DJs also serve alcohol and, depending on the state, may have restrictions regarding employing people under the legal drinking age. However, there are still plenty of places to play besides clubs of this sort, such as school dances, corporate events, and family gatherings.

WHAT EDUCATION AND TRAINING DO INDEPENDENT DISC JOCKEYS NEED?

No formal training is necessary once you purchase equipment, but practice is. Before a hopeful DJ lands a gig, he or she has to know the ins and outs of the equipment. There are a few videos out there that can teach you the basics, or you can ask a friend who has some experience to show you the basics. Once you've got them down, you can have fun developing your own style. This is one field where individuality can really make a difference.

A DJ performs at a nightclub party in Las Vegas. As one song plays, he uses his headphones to listen to and prepare the next song.

Every DJ has his own style and personality. In one technique, a DJ may scratch a vinyl record by moving it back and forth on a turntable.

SALARY EXPECTATIONS

Pay varies for DJs. If you manage to play a considerable amount and make a name for yourself, you can request more money than a DJ who is just starting out. Pay is usually on a per-night basis and is influenced by a large amount of factors, including venue size and attendance. One way to find a basic amount to charge would be to contact other DJs in your area and ask them.

CAREER OUTLOOK

The prognosis for deejaying seems to be very good. Many establishments hire people to play music, and people who host events look for DJs who can help to make their celebrations or gatherings as enjoyable and as memorable as possible.

FOR MORE INFORMATION

ORGANIZATIONS

American Disc Jockey Association
20118 N. 67th Avenue, Suite 300-605
Glendale, AZ 85308
(888) 723-5776
Web site: http://www.adja.org

Canadian Disc Jockey Association
1008 Manchester Road
London, ON N6H 5J1
Canada
(877) 472-0653
Web site: http://www.CDja.org

National Association of Mobile Entertainers
Box 144
Willow Grove, PA 19090
(215) 658-1193
Web site: http://www.nameentertainers.com

Professional DJ Association
Web site: http://prodjassociation.com

BOOKS

Crisell, Luke, Phil White, and Rob Principe. *On the Record: The Scratch DJ Academy Guide*. New York, NY: St. Martin's Press, 2009.
An authoritative guide to the art of deejaying.

Emsley, Jason. *The Laptop DJ Handbook: Set-ups and Techniques of the Modern Performer*. Boston, MA: Course Technology, 2011.
Readers are given fundamental tutorials and creative performance configurations for popular audio software applications.

Shambro, Joe. *How to Start a Home-Based DJ Business*. Guilford, CT: Globe Pequot Press, 2012.
This comprehensive guide gives advice on every aspect of setting up and running a home-based DJ business.

Steventon, John. *DJing for Dummies*. West Sussex, England: John Wiley & Sons, 2010
Great resource for those interested in starting a deejaying career.

PERIODICALS

DJ Times
Web site: http://www.djtimes.com
Trade magazine for professional DJs. Features video
    interviews of top DJs, information about the industry,
    charts, news, and more.

Mobile Beat: The DJ Magazine
Web site: http: http://www.mobilebeat.com
Mobile Beat is dedicated to the specialized interests of
    working mobile entertainers. Each issue is packed
    with coverage and reviews of new equipment and
    music along with tips on how to boost bookings and
    get more referrals from each performance.

WEB SITES

Due to the changing nature of Internet links, Rosen Publishing has developed an online list of Web sites related
to the subject of this book. This site is updated regularly.
Please use this link to access the list:

http://www.rosenlinks.com/CCWC/Music

CHAPTER 10

INSTRUMENT TECH

Instrument techs (or technicians) are people who specialize in one or more types of services that they provide to touring companies. They're often nicknamed roadies, and they are the backbone of musical and theatrical companies that hit the road and travel all over the world to bring entertainment to the public.

A DAY IN THE LIFE

Roadies have training and expertise in certain areas connected with live performances, such as lighting, sound, stage design, and instruments, to name a few. Instrument technicians also support touring musical groups in ways we rarely think of. They take care of costumes and food. They drive the band bus and the truck containing the equipment. Depending on the size of the operation, a crew of instrument technicians can range from two men who are responsible for all of the technical support to hundreds of members of a support staff.

If you decide to become a roadie, you are really becoming a kind of performer. Singers can't be heard if the speakers don't work, and they can't be seen if the spotlights are burnt out. Instrument technicians perform, but they do their best work

where no one in the audience can see them. If you can play an instrument well, but are not interested in being the person in front of the crowd, you may want to try your hand at being an instrument technician. Can't play an instrument? That's not a problem. There are plenty of other jobs that help shows or performances run, so you could see which ones interest you most.

Instrument technicians can obtain work on a local or regional level, as well as on a national level. Local work is close to home and involves helping out local bands or providing technical support for the community theater group. Check local papers and music magazines to see who may need help in your area. The regional level is more involved. First, it involves traveling, which is one way to see another part of the country while you work. Regional tech crews are small (two to three people) and assist bands

Instrument technicians set up the East Room for a White House music series concert. The technicians will make sure everything is working before the show starts.

or touring companies of Broadway shows, for example. Working at the regional level usually requires experience, which can be gained locally. Occasionally, however, regional companies will take on apprentices to train. The national level (sometimes international, too) is where the best technicians find work. At this stage, level of technical skill is very high; the chance to be away for long periods of time is even higher. Some jobs can even involve prolonged travel in another country.

One of the keys to being an instrument technician is dedication. It may take some time to progress from working locally to working nationally, but persistence pays off. The more you work at a local or regional level, the more people you will meet who may be able to help you find work with a traveling company.

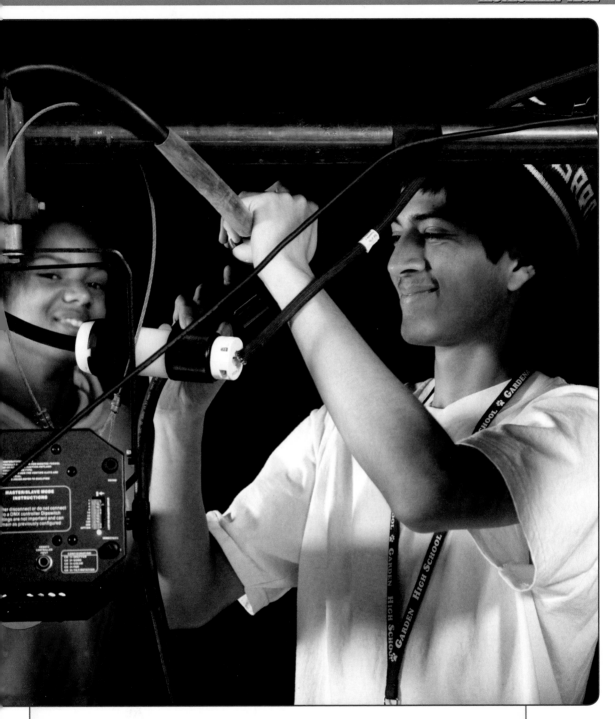

Instrument technicians adjust the equipment backstage. In addition to setting up equipment before a performance, the technicians will provide technical support and troubleshoot any problems during the show.

WHAT EDUCATION AND TRAINING DO INSTRUMENT TECHS NEED?

Unfortunately, there is no such thing as roadie school. To become an instrument technician, start in high school by working as a stagehand for a school or local production to decide whether or not you would like to pursue that sort of work once you graduate. This is a great time to learn the basics and to find out where your talent lies. You can also contact the local branch of the International Alliance of Theatrical Stage Employees (IATSE) or a professional sound and lighting company and intern for them. The more training and/or experience a person gains before finishing high school, the better.

SALARY EXPECTATIONS

The pay varies for each level of work, as well as for particular jobs—some bands or companies may pay more than others. At the regional level, techs usually get paid per gig, so unless you work every night, the work is definitely part-time. As roadies move to higher levels of responsibility, the pay will increase and so will the hours.

THINK ABOUT IT

Traveling and working with a bunch of people for a prolonged period of time means that an instrument technician has to be able to work well with other people. Everyone who works for a band or on the crew of a touring show should have the same goal—the best performance possible every time. And tours can go on for months. Sometimes your ability to get along with people may be just as valuable as the technical skill you've been hired for. Being stuck on a bus with the same people for months is a skill in itself. The work is hard but rewarding if you ultimately want the chance to travel and live a different lifestyle. If you don't feel that you could be a team player, then this may not be the job for you.

FOR MORE INFORMATION

ORGANIZATIONS

The ESTA Foundation
620 Ninth Avenue, Suite 609
New York, NY 10036
(212) 244-1421
Web site: http://www.estafoundation.org

The International Alliance of Theatrical Stage Employees (IATSE), Moving Picture Technicians, Artists and Allied Crafts
1430 Broadway, 20th Floor
New York, NY 10018
(212) 730-1770
Web site: http://www.iatse-intl.org.

Musical Instrument Technicians Association
Web site: http://www.mitatechs.org

Occupational Safety & Health Administration (OSHA)
200 Constitution Avenue
Washington, DC 20210
(800) 321-OSHA (6742)
Web site: http://www.osha.gov

BOOKS

Hince, Peter. *Queen Unseen: My Life with the Greatest Rock Band of the 20th Century*. London, UK: John Black Publishing, 2011.
For more than a decade, author Peter Hince toured the world and headed up the road crew for rock band Queen.

McGinn, Matt. *Roadie: My Life on the Road with Coldplay*. London, UK: Anova Books, 2010.
An insider's guide that is filled with tour stories about daily roadie duties.

Waddell, Ray, Rich Barnett, and Jake Berry. *This Business of Concert Promotion and Touring: A Practical Guide to Creating, Selling, Organizing, and Staging Concerts*. New York, NY: Billboard Books, 2007.
Addresses the business of concerts—from creating a show, to selling it, organizing, and staging it.

Wright, James "Tappy." *Rock Roadie: Backstage and Confidential with Hendrix, Elvis, the Animals, Tina Turner, and an All-Star Cast*. New York, NY: St. Martin's Press, 2009.
Written by a roadie for some legendary music stars, the book takes you behind the scenes on the road.

PERIODICALS

Pollstar
Web site: http://www.pollstar.com
A print magazine with an online component, *Pollstar*
   publishes concert tour schedules for music professionals.

WEB SITES

Due to the changing nature of Internet links, Rosen Publishing has developed an online list of Web sites related
to the subject of this book. This site is updated regularly.
Please use this link to access the list:

http://www.rosenlinks.com/CCWC/Music

CHAPTER 11

RECORD COMPANY EMPLOYEE

Record companies deal with what everyone wants to hear: music. In some ways, record companies form the center of the music industry as we know it today. Recorded sound accounts for a great deal of employment opportunities. Record companies are responsible for the recording, promotion, and supply of various projects from a variety of musicians and singers. There are dozens and dozens of jobs in this field—some record companies occupy two or three floors in an office building! We'll focus on the positions that you're more likely to obtain soon after high school.

A DAY IN THE LIFE

Every person who works at a record company is very important to the end goal—getting music to the general public—and positions are usually available at lower levels. The lowest of these involves working on what is called a street team. Street teams are assembled by employees of a record company to perform a series of special tasks that the record company employees may not be able to perform. These tasks may include:

hanging posters, handing out flyers and stickers, or other promotions to generate buzz on the street for an artist. Street team jobs are part-time and primarily intended for high school and college students.

Other entry-level positions that you might try are intern positions or campus representatives. A campus rep is a student hired to set up promotional displays or hand out flyers on campus. Often they work for little to no pay, setting up merchandising booths and selling artist T-shirts, stickers, buttons, pins, and posters. They might also set up a point-of-purchase display, which contains CDs, videos, and other pieces of merchandise. Still, even though they aren't making a lot of money, they are gaining experience and making contacts that can help them move up the chain to a better job in the future.

Interns can do a variety of tasks, from large to small, at a record company. They might not get paid much, or maybe not at all, but they gain valuable experience and make contacts for the future. Interns perform many of the same jobs as other staff members, which gives them a fantastic opportunity for hands-on experience. Nearly every department hires interns, so you can get experience in a variety of positions and departments.

Working in an unpaid or low-paying position such as a street team, campus rep, or intern can open up a lot of doors in your music career. You'll get to know quite a few people at a record company; this is important if a paid position opens up. That first paid position might not be glamorous—it might even be in the company mailroom. But like any entry-level position, think of it as a step in the door. Pay your dues, get to know the people and how the company runs, and you'll be putting yourself in a great position if a better job opens up. Many record company promotions come from within, and you'll be at the heart of the company, seeing how all departments operate. Sometimes, if you know you want to work for a record company, but you're unsure about what you actually want to do, this can give you a taste of different jobs without committing to them.

Perform well in your first entry-level job and you'll probably be moving up as soon as something opens up. You might try the job of a merchandising coordinator, which involves doing everything needed to get the posters and flyers and checklists to the street teams. Merchandising coordinators are given a small budget by their superiors to complete these tasks, and it is often very challenging to do so. Merchandising coordinators report to product development representatives (PDRs). PDRs may be placed in charge of a certain record or artist, and it's their job to publicize a record to get the word out and get people into the stores. PDRs may work on one record or artist at a time, concentrating only on that project. At other times, PDRs may have ten priorities to divide their time among, which is usually the case.

A record company employee removes vinyl records from a press at a production facility. In recent years, the production of vinyl records has fallen with more people buying digital downloads of music.

WHAT EDUCATION AND TRAINING DO RECORD COMPANY EMPLOYEES NEED?

No formal education is necessary. Out of all of the professions in this guide, the recording industry probably has the largest amount of employees who did not go to college to train for their job. Colleges don't offer record company degrees, which helps to make the playing field more even. Hard work is very important once you get your foot in the door in the record industry. Individuals who volunteer for tough assignments or harder jobs with longer hours are the employees who learn more at a quicker rate. They are also the ones who are easier to remember when promotion time rolls around. Be motivated! Pay your dues now and you'll reap the rewards later.

SALARY EXPECTATIONS

Salaries depend on the specific job. A person who works on a street team, as an intern, or as a campus rep usually will not get paid, but some companies do offer a minimal amount to individuals who hang posters or hand out flyers to advertise a record label's product. Entry-level positions, such as in the mailroom, generally have low salaries. As you advance through the company, your pay will also increase. Plus you may be able to score some perks such as concert tickets or other merchandise.

CAREER OUTLOOK

There is a high amount of turnover at record companies, especially in lower-level positions. If one company doesn't have a need for interns, keep looking—odds are there is work to be found. As with other jobs involving music, you may want to combine your work at a record company with another job until you begin to move up in the ranks.

ADDITIONAL INFORMATION

Start small. The smaller the company, the fewer employees there are. This means that it will be easier to be known around the office and receive more responsibility at an earlier

Record company employees have fun at a live concert. One of the perks of the job is being able to get concert tickets to see the latest bands and artists.

point in your job. You should also be hopeful, yet realistic. Understand that it may be a long time before you are out on the road, scouting out small towns for the next big band.

Record companies are open during the day, but musicians mostly play at night. If you think that working with record labels and artists is for you, remember that it involves working during the day and usually spending some of your "off" time working. You may have to attend a concert to help ensure a band's show runs smoothly or stay later than normal to get a large mailing together or to work on a flyer to distribute to street teams. The music industry is a busy one, especially when you work at a record company. Be prepared to throw away your idea of a traditional nine-to-five schedule.

Also remember that the music business is always changing. If you can think of a job that hasn't been created yet, invent it yourself. Innovation is one of the hallmarks of the business.

FOR MORE INFORMATION

ORGANIZATIONS

Academy of Country Music
5500 Balboa Boulevard
Encino, CA 91316
(818) 788-9136
Web site: http://www.acmcountry.com

Creative Musicians Coalition
1-24 W. Willcox Avenue
Peoria, IL 61604
(309) 685-4843
Web site: http://www.aimcmc.com

National Association of Record Industry Professionals
P.O. Box 2446
Toluca Lake, CA 91610
(818) 769-7007
Web site: http://www.narip.com

Recording Industry Association of America (RIAA)
1025 F St. NW, 10th Floor
Washington, DC 20004
(202) 775-0101
Web site: http://www.riaa.com

BOOKS

Davis, Clive. *The Soundtrack of My Life*. New York, NY: Simon & Schuster, 2013.
Autobiography of a record industry legend.

Macy, Amy, Tom Hutchinson, and Paul Allen. *Record Label Marketing*. Burlington, MA: Focal Press, 2010.
A comprehensive look at the inner workings of record labels.

Mottola, Tommy. *Hitmaker: The Man and His Music*. New York, NY: Hachette Book Group, 2013.
Autobiography of one of the most successful executives in the history of the music industry.

Wilentz, Sean. 360 *Sound: The Columbia Records Story*. San Francisco, CA: Chronicle Books: 2012.
The history of one of the greatest record labels in the United States.

PERIODICALS

Pollstar
Web site: http://www.pollstar.com

A print magazine with an online component, *Pollstar* publishes concert tour schedules for music professionals.

WEB SITES

Due to the changing nature of Internet links, Rosen Publishing has developed an online list of Web sites related to the subject of this book. This site is updated regularly. Please use this link to access the list:

http://www.rosenlinks.com/CCWC/Music

CHAPTER 12

ARTIST BOOKING AGENT

Live music is a popular and important form of entertainment for both spectators and performers. Music fans go to clubs and stadiums to see bands perform live. Talent scouts in the entertainment business often travel to live events to see artists they may want to sign. Musicians themselves tour to make an important portion of their income. Who makes sure that all of these people have a place to go? A booking agent.

A DAY IN THE LIFE

The main job of a booking agent is to handle engagements for the artists and groups he or she represents. If working with an up-and-coming but unknown band, the booking agent will have to work hard to book engagements. If the artist is well known and already has a fan following, the booking agent may help the artist decide which engagements to book. In a typical day, a booking agent may spend seven to eight hours on the phone trying to sell acts to venues, promoters, and club managers and negotiating contract terms.

An artist booking agent talks with a band's manager as they perform at a music festival. Many booking agents use festivals to promote artists they have already signed.

After a booking agent makes an agreement for an artist to appear, he or she prepares and sends out a contract that will be signed by the promoter, club manager, or other person who booked the artist to perform. The contract should include specific information about the engagement, including dates, times, number of performances, payment amount, payment terms, and other conditions.

Some booking agents work for large agencies. In a company with many agents, you may specialize in a certain type of artist or genre of music. For example, one agent may represent classical music acts. Another may represent country bands. Regardless, they are expected to work with the artist's manager and record company to decide which appearances and concerts will be the best for promoting the artist's music.

Booking agents are often looking for hot, new talent to represent. To find these diamonds, they may hold auditions for potential artists and groups. Often, booking agents will also attend music showcases and clubs around the country, all in the search for the next great talent. A booking agent can have more than one client; in fact, they can have as many acts as they can juggle and still represent each effectively. Sometimes, they will even represent acts that are competitors with each other! Agents want to sign as many clients as they can. The more clients they have, the more money they can make.

WHAT EDUCATION AND TRAINING DO BOOKING AGENTS NEED?

There is no school that can teach you how to be a booking agent. You might want to take a seminar, workshop, or course

A booking agent talks on the phone to set up appearances for his clients. Once an engagement has been agreed upon, he will talk with club managers to negotiate contract terms.

in booking entertainment. Courses and seminars in contracts and contract law are also helpful.

Although a formal education isn't necessary, booking agents must be salespeople at heart. Their success depends on their ability to sell an artist or group to someone who is looking to book a concert. Often they must be aggressive, calling people on the phone and constantly following up and pushing their clients. And no matter how well you plan, at some point, something unexpected will happen. Maybe a group will cancel an appearance at the last minute or a club manager will try to pay less money than originally promised. Regardless, booking agents must be able to work under pressure and keep their cool no matter what the situation.

SALARY EXPECTATIONS

Booking agents are usually paid by commission. They get a percentage of the artists' fees. If the agent works for an agency, they may also get a base salary plus a commission for their bookings. The more acts an agent can handle and the more events he or she books, the more money the agent will make.

CAREER OUTLOOK

As long as people still want to hear live music, there will be a need for people to coordinate their performances. The easiest way to break into the business may be by booking local talent at local clubs and venues. From there, agents can advance to booking in a wider region and booking larger acts. With experience, the agent may be able to move from a regional agency to a larger national agency.

FOR MORE INFORMATION

ORGANIZATIONS

American Federation of Musicians (AFM)
1501 Broadway, Suite 600
New York, NY 10036
(212) 869-1330
Web site: http://www.afm.org

Association of Talent Agents
9255 Sunset Boulevard, Suite 930
Los Angeles, CA 90069
(310) 274-0628
Web site: http://www.agentassociation.com

National Association of Recording Merchandisers (NARM)
9 Eves Drive, Suite 120
Marlton, NJ 08053
(856) 596-2221
Web site: http://www.narm.com

North American Performing Arts Managers and Agents
459 Columbus Avenue, #133
New York, NY 10024
(800) 867-3281
Web site: http://www.napama.org

BOOKS

Allen, Paul. *Artist Management for the Music Business.*
Burlington, MA: Focal Press, 2011.
Clear, in-depth information on how to work in artist
management.

Goldstein, Jeri. *How to Be Your Own Booking Agent: The
Musician's & Performing Artist's Guide to Successful
Touring.* Palmyra, VA: The New Music Times, Inc., 2008.
A top-selling music and performing-arts business book,
packed with advice, methods, and action plans for the
musician and artist.

Reynolds, Andy. *The Tour Book: How to Get Your Music
on the Road.* Boston, MA: Course Technology, 2008.
This book gives practical advice, hints, and tips on every
part of putting on a live show, including show booking and promotion from an industry professional.

Waddell, Ray, Rich Barnett, and Jake Berry. *This Business
of Concert Promotion and Touring: A Practical Guide
to Creating, Selling, Organizing, and Staging Concerts.*
New York, NY: Billboard Books, 2007.
Addresses the business of concerts—from creating a
show, to selling it, organizing, and staging it.

PERIODICALS

Pollstar
Web site: http://www.pollstar.com
A print magazine with an online component, *Pollstar*
    publishes concert tour schedules for music profes-
    sionals.

WEB SITES

Due to the changing nature of Internet links, Rosen Publishing has developed an online list of Web sites related
to the subject of this book. This site is updated regularly.
Please use this link to access the list:

http://www.rosenlinks.com/CCWC/Music

GLOSSARY

AUDIO ENGINEER A person who designs or operates sound recording and reproduction equipment.

BOOK To schedule a band or artist to play live music in a venue.

CLIPS Published writing samples.

COMMISSION A percentage of the profit earned by a performance, artist, or recording.

FEEDBACK The high-pitched output that often occurs when someone speaks into a microphone.

FORMAT The type of music a radio station plays.

FREE-FORM Describes a radio station that plays music across all genres and doesn't stick to one format.

LABEL An individual record company or one of several product names under which a record company releases its recordings.

MERCHANDISING Any product that uses an artist's image, name, or likeness for promotion.

MIXING BOARD Equipment used by a DJ or a sound engineer that combines and adjust sounds from different sources; also called a mixer.

MUSIC NOTATION The written language of music.

PLAYLIST A list of songs that the music director of a radio station has determined will be played by the station's disc jockeys.

PORTFOLIO A collection of an applicant's work (usually writing samples or art pieces) that serves as a sort of résumé.

REPERTOIRE The group of songs that a singer or musician is prepared to perform.

RESIDENCY A regular, long-term gig for a band or DJ to perform in a venue.

ROADIE Also known as instrument technician, this person prepares the set for a musician, band, or show by tuning the instruments, checking the sound, and doing other tasks that contribute to the success of a production.

SHOWCASE A short performance where an artist auditions for invited industry and label representatives in the hopes of gaining a record contract.

STREET TEAM A group of unpaid people hired by a record company to promote a musician or band at the street level.

INDEX

ABOUT THE AUTHOR

Carla Mooney is a graduate of the University of Pennsylvania. She writes for young people and is the author of numerous educational books. She has played the piano since the third grade and has experimented with the clarinet, violin, and guitar. She enjoys listening to and creating music every day.

PHOTO CREDITS

Cover, pp. 3, 7 iStockphoto.com/Chris Schmidt; p. 9 auremar/Shutterstock.com; pp. 12–13 KidStock/Blend Images/Getty Images; p. 21 Jeffrey Ufberg/WireImage/Getty Images; p. 23 Bob Daemmrich/The Image Works; p. 26 Rob Marmion/Shutterstock.com; p. 33 ronstik/Shutterstock.com; pp. 36–37 iStockphoto.com/Andrey Tsidvintsev; pp. 44–45 Dream Pictures/Blend Images/Getty Images; pp. 48–49 iStockphoto/Thinkstock; p. 55 Brian Chase/Shutterstock.com; pp. 56–57 Pavel L Photo and Video/Shutterstock.com; p. 59 Ysbrand Cosijn/Shutterstock.com; pp. 66–67 altrendo images/Getty Images; pp. 70–71 Antonio Scorza/AFP/Getty Images; pp. 78–79 Michael Buckner/Getty Images; pp. 80–81 © AP Images; p. 87 D Dipasupil/Getty Images; pp. 90–91 Jon Furniss/WireImage/Getty Images; pp. 92–93 © Santa Rosa Press/ZUMA Press; p. 100 © iStockphoto.com/Oktay Ortakcioglu; p. 102 Bryan Steffy/Getty Images; pp. 104–105 dpaint/Shutterstock.com; pp. 110–111 Getty Images; pp. 112–113 Blend Images/SuperStock; pp. 122–123 Bloomberg/Getty Images; p.125 Brand New Images/Iconica/Getty Images; p. 131 Ben Sklar/The New York Times/Redux; p. 133 Purestock/Thinkstock; cover and interior design elements © iStockphoto.com/pialhovik (banner); © iStockphoto.com/David Shultz (dots), Melamory/Shutterstock.com (hexagon pattern), Lost & Taken (boxed text background texture), bioraven/Shutterstock.com (chapter opener pages icons).

Designer: Michael Moy; Editor: Bethany Bryan;
Photo Researcher: Marty Levick